PRAISE FOR
FEBRUARIES

"*februaries* by Michele Evans is a compilation of eleven years of Black History Month reflections in verse, highlighting celebrated authors, thinkers, poets, and artists. Written in a voice steeped in the heartbreaking dynamic that is being Black in America, Evans' one-of-a-kind style sings like a canary in the coal mine, warning us of the dangers of losing our humanity and urging us to see each other with gentleness and grace. *februaries* meets this moment, inspiring us to think, act, and speak about the injustices of our time."

Rowana Abbensetts-Dobson, author of *Departure Story*, founder of Spoken Black Girl, and Editor-in-Chief of *Spoken Black Girl Magazine*

~

"Every poem in *februaries* is a tribute, a heartbreak, a moment to pause and catch your breath. Michele Evans always devastates me! I'll be thinking about this book for a long time."

Hannah Grieco, author of *First Kicking, Then Not*

~

"*februaries* is a touching, honorific, and nimble collection of verse. The poet, Michele Evans, marvelously commands a variety of forms, including eintou, triolet, cento, ghazal, blackout, and double golden shovel. Through it all, the words sing and sharply remind us of history and precarity—and also love."

Keith Gilyard, author of *Impressions: New and Selected Poems*

~

februaries

by
Michele Evans

YELLOW ARROW
PUBLISHING
Baltimore, Maryland, USA

Library of Congress Control Number: 2026933073
ISBN (paperback): 978-1-967202-01-0

Epigraph source: National African American Read-In web page
(ncte.org/get-involved/african-american-read-in). © 2025 by the
National Council of Teachers of English. Used with permission.

Cover and interior art by Harrison Evans (Instagram
@yatsby_happy999). Cover design by Alexa Laharty (Instagram
@alexaelisabeth). Headshot on back cover by Kendall Evans
(Instagram @snapsbykee44). Interior design by Yellow Arrow
Publishing. For more information, see yellowarrowpublishing.com.

For Elizabeth Hawkins Matthews
and Ruth Peterson Stancil
and all the ancestors

"It is important for all of us to see ourselves in books."

Dr. Jerrie Cobb Scott
founder of the National African American Read-In

CONTENTS

preface   3

2015
to rewrite this world again   7
muse   9
no. 1   11

2016
at midnight, apartment 1 sits by the window,   15
    still waits for her ghost to come home
swan song   17
no. 2   19

2017
haiku blues   23
iconic   25
no. 3   27

2018
an american girl   31
≤: less than or equal to?   33
no. 4   35

2019
can i buy a vowel?   39
objects in the mirror are closer than they appear   41
no. 5   43

2020
sugar plum   47
her name is   49
no. 6   51

2021
enjambment   55
still   57
no. 7   59

2022
spiraling   63
dark, and lovely, and limitless   65
no. 8   67

2023
the daily mad lib   71
973.0496   73
no. 9   75

2024
three tercets to remember   79
run the "gambit"   81
no. 10   83

2025
fsbo: 5416 second street, northwest   87
in memoriam   89
no. 11   93

<u>postlude</u>
acknowledgments   97
in gratitude   102
about the artist   104
about the author   105

februaries

PREFACE

In February 1990 the first National African American Read-In was established by the Black Caucus of the National Council of Teachers of English (NCTE). Twenty-five years after the inaugural event, the English Department at Broad Run High School in Loudoun County, Virginia, where I have taught for more than two decades, held our first read-in on February 25, 2015, to celebrate Black History Month. Its purpose was threefold: (1) to foster an appreciation of literature, (2) to shine a literary spotlight on favorite African American authors, and (3) to create valuable learning experiences leading to stimulating conversations about literacy and diversity.

Tinesha Davis, the author of *All Black Girls Ain't Got No Rhythm and other urban hymns* (Magic People Press, 2006) and writing coach for Book-in-a-Day, a nonprofit program that teaches high school students how to write poetry and publish a book in a day, was invited to be our guest speaker. After sharing writing anecdotes and reciting poems to a standing room only crowd in the school's choral room, Tinesha Davis celebrated and encouraged all students and staff to read poetry and prose written by writers from the African diaspora.

That year I read "muse," an original poem about finding the courage to write again, to the audience. For the next ten Februaries, from 2016 to 2025, I wrote a new poem before the school's annual celebration and another one afterward to honor that year's guest. It wasn't until I began working on *purl* (Finishing Line Press, 2025), my first poetry collection, that I realized I had a second collection forming.

2015

AFRICAN AMERICAN READ-IN

SPECIAL GUEST

TINESHA DAVIS

TO REWRITE THIS WORLD AGAIN

For Tinesha Davis

she is
so genuine
a prized african queen,
muse painting our world in black
stories with her inked pen
a realm of love
not hate.

MUSE

For Maya Angelou

she was the tenth one. the one i added to the original,
classical, mythological greek nine. she was a civil rights
activist, a leading hollywood actress, a pulitzer-prize
(winning) presidential inaugurating artist. she was
loveliest among goddesses, a heavenly angel, a once
muted and caged bird now free, a phenomenal woman, a
creative inspiration, a lyrical calliope. you see before
invoking her, i had this problem. and this problem had me.

i was unable to see, brooding in a black box
—blinded and belittled, badgered and blacklisted.

i was unable to hear, drowning in a black sea
—deflated and damaged, drained and devalued.

i was unable to feel, wrestling in a black hole
—weakened and wounded, withered and wronged.

i was unable to think, suffocating in a black smoke
—stereotyped and smothered, scarred and second-guessed.

i was unable to speak, muttering in a black tongue
—marginalized and muzzled, muted and misunderstood.

i was unable to write, outlining in a black book
—obstructed and omitted, oppressed and objectified.

but now when she sings in me and through me that
heavy shroud of ebony and obscurity is miraculously lifted.
and those shadows—the dark ones lurking in my mind and
heart—completely vanish
so i can see, and hear, and feel, and think, and
speak, and finally write again.

NO. 1

our own rhythm is a thing of beauty
poems
sing
dance
breathe
poems
holler
praise
comfort
poems
a thing of rhythm is our own beauty

2016

AFRICAN AMERICAN READ-IN

SPECIAL GUEST

LE HINTON

AT MIDNIGHT, APARTMENT 1 SITS BY THE WINDOW, STILL WAITS FOR HER GHOST TO COME HOME

For Le Hinton and Breonna Taylor

because breonna's now knocking on heaven's door
she will never stabilize, transport, or save another life
in louisville, kentucky's latest casualty of war
because breonna's now knocking on heaven's door
there to meet others like freddie from baltimore
this black daughter will never be a nurse or a wife
because breonna's now knocking on heaven's door
she will never stabilize, transport, or save another life

SWAN SONG

For Kennedy and Harrison

each time he walks out my front door wearing
a bullseye, i think, *will it be for the last time*?

each time he walks out my front door wearing
a permanent tattoo, i hear an anthem—a broken
record looping in my head.

each time he walks out my front door wearing
his birthmark, bobbing his head from side to side,
a different jam blaring from his beats, i fear the worst.

each time he walks out my front door wearing
this target on his back, i wish i could download
a different track for him. but in my country 'tis
of thee, sweet land of liberty, you hear about sons
that look like him.

sons that wear the same bullseye on their backs.

sons that walk out front doors, say bye
to their mamas and never come back.

sons whose last breaths, moments, and verses
become lyrics of a swan song remix played
on heavy rotation across this nation, a tune
as old as itself, and it goes a little something like this:

sanford's trayvon asked,
     what are you following me for?
ferguson's michael insisted,
     i don't have a gun. stop shooting.
baltimore's freddie gasped,
     i can't breathe. i need a pump.

each time another black son walks out
his mama's front door for the last time, these verses strike
a chord in many of us, but why not all of us?
can we lift every voice to write a new song
that rings with the harmonies of liberties?

he is
still walking out my front door,
still wearing his bullseye,
still wearing his permanent tattoo,
still wearing this target on his back,
each time i pray it's not his last.

NO. 2

empty, i hid in the silent pages
channeling
patuxent
piano keys
pittsburgh
channeling
prayers
paris
photographs
channeling
the silent i hid in empty pages

2017

AFRICAN AMERICAN READ-IN

SPECIAL GUEST

VENUS THRASH

HAIKU BLUES

For Venus Thrash (1969–2021)

sweet mister sits back
stage for his lady day who
sings and swings in tune

for sale: gardenia
blooms so big they hide her holes
and stench of burnt hair

you go to my head
when you're smiling them their eyes
pennies from heaven

trauma begets pain
detoxing in solitude
abuse fills her veins

ICONIC

For Billie Holiday

her photograph filtered through a lens
of weary blues, cropped and photoshopped
until it was brand new

until finally erased because that's where
memories lie because erasing words
is easier than understanding why

sweet gardenia blossoms tucked inside
her curly crown masquerade the strange
fruit from poplar trees in town

smoky riffs form notes flowing freely
from her voice, unspeakable lyrics protesting
blacks stripped of choice

a pair of beautiful brown eyes sparkle
under the spotlight hiding her painful
trepidation, retaliation, and stage fright.

NO. 3

but none of us is spared the hard fall from grace
even
eve
aphrodite
mabel
even
shirley
billie
aretha
even
the hard fall but none of us is spared from grace

2018

AFRICAN AMERICAN READ-IN

SPECIAL GUEST

BROOKE C. OBIE

AN AMERICAN GIRL

For Brooke C. Obie

abducted under a moonlit sky as yawning tobacco
    vines perfume the night air of a tiny attic
bedroom where she once slept in a handcrafted
    cradle, woven out of dried willow branches, the
color of ash from cold embers blanketing the
    hearth's floor. her mother, just a chile herself who
dreamt about magical trips north to the city of
    brotherly love and mountains of the granite state,
enchanted worlds where all people live free. the
    cradle, now barren, unleashed waterfall tears
from her dark eyes, as she rocked back and forth on
    her heels, inconsolable, humming
gon' my baby, she gon'. alone, she wandered the
    farm's forty acres on foot before finally enlisting
her folk to help form a search party for her missing
    babe. when her granny refused, no one could
imagine that an elder would be the culprit, the one
    responsible for stealing and killing a mama's
joy. but granny was different, raised in an era of
    partus sequitur ventrem, a time when everybody
knew babies of brown mamas didn't inherit
    privilege from white fathers, indentured servants,
loathsome masters. like a nana from a different era,
    she didn't approve of her granddaughter

mothering a baby named addy, short for addis not
    addison. it was a problem then, and it's still one
now. she and her ilk couldn't overlook that baby's
    cocoa brown skin under the bubblegum pink overcoat
or pleated dress the shade of virginia
    bluebells. nana said matter of factly, *you should*
play with your own kind. she of all people should
    know that history has a way of repeating itself,
quick to judge others, wonder what she would have
    to say about her own childhood playmate, a
real-life living doll. wasn't her skin brown, too?
    wonder how much nana knew about ona judge,
seventeen-year-old slave of the first president, who
    ran away because she was tired of being
trapped, life as a playmate or someone's servant.
    when will society understand there is nothing
unpleasant about little white girls carrying black
    dolls and little black girls carrying white dolls?
vines from the tobacco jasmine are blooming again,
    the wind carries their scent through the
willows that whisper messages from ancestors,
    voices who speak wisdom and truth about
xenophobia and all its dangers to life, liberty, and
    the pursuit of happiness. we must listen to the
young people of america, from alexandria to zion,
    so we always have freedom, truth, love, and
zero tolerance for hatred in all its forms.

≤: LESS THAN OR EQUAL TO?

For Harriet Tubman

i.
what lies beneath, lurking amongst the shadows?
a figure hidden, a single shape shrouded under
a canopy of rope vines, submerged in a pool
of ebony waters, spotlighted under tiny flecks
of patterned moonlight? look closely, and you
might see the conductor's inked silhouette.

ii.
this conductor does not punch tickets—wrinkled
slips peeking out from wholly pockets, disguised
as a shopping list reminder to pick up two bags
of red-skinned potatoes and one large, clove-
studded rosy ham, a mere piece of parchment
to present if pressed by a master in search
of a band of runaways or their sympathizers.

iii.
this conductor does not yell *all aboard* or blow
whistles, or usher families of men, women,
and children up platforms and through train doors,
or hush a trio of voices: lost noises, mistaken
for rustling amber sighs, sinking onyx whispers,
falling crystal murmurs, a melody of silence
and susurrus.

iv.
this conductor does not leave tracks, no splattering
of invisible footprints, two-by-two fading
impressions, buried in the undergrowth
of pearlescent cotton bolls and towering cornstalks
of gilded tobacco, no tracks from steely rails hauling
cargo between untenanted stations and hollowed-
out depots, no tracks to be sniffed out by a quad
of bloodthirsty hounds stopping at river's edge
to watch scented trails wade away.

v.
this conductor does not wonder how black skies
above can be so spacious, so shiny when the land
in between is so spiteful. this conductor does not lose
faith, does not stop moving, climbing, trekking weekly,
painstakingly slow, looking for abolitionists and allies
while also running away from auctioneers
and adversaries.

vi.
so when the rain pummels, and the fire burns,
and the wind smacks, and the snow pounds,
and the overseer strikes, this conductor knows
she must be greater than the rest, knows she must
be fearless, boundless, tireless, selfless because
freedom means nothing to one until it means
everything to all.

NO. 4

a friend can be found even in a strange land
because
felled
trees
sprout
because
twisted
roots
flourish
because
even in a strange land a friend can be found

2019

AFRICAN AMERICAN READ-IN

SPECIAL GUEST

CAMISHA L. JONES

CAN I BUY A VOWEL?

For Camisha L. Jones

"Being hard of hearing is kinda like filling in the blanks
of a Wheel of Fortune puzzle."
"The Sound Barrier" by Camisha L. Jones

in mom_nts lik_ th_s_

fuel_d by str_ss

r_m_b_r to br_ath_

strik_ anxi_ty

b_li_v_ in grac_

smil_ th_n pr_t_nd

wh_n_v_r

flar_s r_ignit_

b_for_ th_ir pr_s_nc_

smold_ring _mb_rs

r_fus_ to b_ _xtinguish_d

_v_n wh_n th_y whisp_r.

OBJECTS IN THE MIRROR ARE CLOSER
THAN THEY APPEAR

each time the thought
is always the same:

*just make it
home safely.*

navigating
foggy tunnels,
dark alleys,
dead-end streets,

seeing lights
flashing blue
first before
siren sounds
follow.

still afraid, triggered
by a few bad apples
wearing uniforms
so dark they're
almost invisible

trying to turn
chaos into order

a natural reflex
hands in plain sight,
with a mind of their own,
they betray and tremble
the baton
breaks the glass
just as a faceless man
in the window says,
license and registration!

the baton
breaks the glass
just as a faceless man
in the window
says, *license and registration?*

a natural reflex:
hands in plain sight!

with a mind
of their own,
they betray
and tremble
trying to

turn chaos
into order.

still afraid,
triggered by
a few bad apples
wearing uniforms
so dark, they're
almost invisible

navigating foggy
tunnels, dark alleys,
dead-end streets,
seeing lights
flashing
blue first before
siren sounds follow

each time, the thought
is always the same:
*just make it
home safely.*

NO. 5

their chant for a moment becomes still as a whisper
despite
beeping
chirping
ringing
despite
knocking
clattering
blaring
despite
their chant for a moment becomes still as a whisper

2020

AFRICAN AMERICAN READ-IN

SPECIAL GUEST

DR. JOANNE V. GABBIN

SUGAR PLUM

For Dr. Joanne V. Gabbin

the second we locked eyes, i searched for your name,
your tender skin sticky, the color of candied rhubarb.

stuck next door listening for the sound of tender cries,
waiting for the nurse to bring a seven-pound delivery.

the patient nurse waited more than seven minutes after the delivery
so i could snuggle with you, my sweet little dumpling, one last time.

the moment your sweet little dumpling cheek stroked mine,
visions of your loving and caring first mother danced in my head.

wet cheeks nestled in an empty bed, visions of my first loving moments
as your mother, ten tiny fingers, tightly closed, yet still caressing my heart.

ten tiny fingers now play open close them when she says hi, bye,
or calls you the apple of her eye, sugar lump, or sweet potato pie.

sugar lump, sweet potato pie, dumpling, the sweetest under the sun,
the second we locked eyes, i knew your name had to be sugar plum.

HER NAME IS

i don't understand, twenty-four hours. i can't wait
that long. she isn't lost. she wouldn't run away. she's been
taken, kidnapped, stolen, abducted, and she's scared.
i know she wants to be found. why aren't you saying
anything? you have to help me find her.

her name is . . .

where is your outrage? what if it were your daughter?
your sister? cousin? niece? grandchild? i just can't stand
here wasting any more time, i should be out there right
now looking for her. you should be out there looking
for her. we should be out there together, looking for her,
before it's too late.

her name is . . .

where is her video footage? what do you mean someone
didn't do anything about the blinking red light
from the convenience store security camera,
didn't notice it dangling precariously from the ceiling,
didn't bother to change the dead double-a batteries inside,
didn't realize it was supposed to record her first frantic moments
not her last.

her name is . . .

where is her missing person poster? what do you mean
someone didn't look carefully while waiting in line
for a price adjustment, didn't see her faded and dated
black-and-white photograph, didn't notice her buried
underneath other forgotten faces plastered on a filthy
store wall next to product recalls and equal opportunity
notices, didn't realize her story was only being broadcast
at a customer service center near you.

her name is . . .

where is her amber alert? what do you mean someone
didn't listen for her muted screams coming from
the trunk of a car with a rattling exhaust pipe, didn't notice
the vehicle with the broken taillight traveling the wrong
way on a dark, dead-end street, didn't bother to write
down the three letters and numbers that were supposed
to save her life.

her name is . . .

we must do better. we must find her before it's too late.

her name, you ask?
her name is . . .
her   name   is

humanity.

NO. 6

poetry was a way to tell the truth and a tool to change society
blooming
couplets
golden
crowns
blooming
violets
furious
voices
blooming
poetry was a way to change society and a tool to tell the truth

2021

AFRICAN AMERICAN READ-IN

SPECIAL GUEST

REUBEN JACKSON

ENJAMBMENT

For Reuben Jackson (1956–2024)

do i pretend
i don't see

other people
pretending
not to see

us as dapper
as the evening
sky i nod to

the moon
with a posse
of teardrops
i can't count

that high spent
nearly every
saturday
at the one
step down

brilliant brown
voices of
my youth

love walked in
so did poetry

the sweet
obvious medley
memory is kind
of a jukebox

don't be afraid
push the buttons

STILL

if music really is our universal language,
then why does it feel like we are still
stuck in the thirties picking cotton to play
cotton, still consulting green travel books to exit
our front doors only to enter their back doors,
still stuck on stage, never in seats of smoky cafés
and cabarets, safe? places and spaces where ebony keys
perfect harmonies only for ivory, where blue note trills
spill from a legendary monk, duke, or prince
whose colored strokes hit different still
where composed and indisposed steely patrons
sit stony, still tone deaf, so whack no auto-tune
could repair their sharp hands crossed not clapping, flat feet
crossed not tapping, where minds, hearts, and body parts
are still shackling us to black pasts, unchanged
by melodies, still waving checkered flags while crooning
checkmate, still stealing inventions for patents once
denied, still refereeing rolling dice betting on highs
never lows, still blocking minors from pitching majors,
where minds, hearts, and body parts appear still
even though under inky skies their shadows sway
and spin dancing near secret stills to our jigs
on the b-sides, intervals of improvisation, accidental
collaborations, opal and obsidian juxtapositions
of a tune called life. so, tell me, if music really is our
universal language, then why does it feel like we are
still still . . .

NO. 7

a falsetto is sunlight set to music
when
doves
cry
like
when
clouds
rain
purple
when
music is sunlight set to a falsetto

2022

AFRICAN AMERICAN READ-IN

SPECIAL GUEST

DINAHSTA "MISS KIANE" THOMAS

SPIRALING

For Miss Kiane

back in the day, up and down city street tree lines,
girls like me stutter step over chalky hopscotch lines

brown skinned, red palmed, neck snapping, gum popping,
one jumper and two turners swinging, all singing lines

about a woman named miss mary mack dressed in black
with silver buttons all down her back, rhyming lines

easier to remember than keeping your arms to the side
while rocking back and forth between threaded lines

and spidery shadows where the rope doesn't catch your feet
or anxious shoelaces threatening to tangle parallel lines

better time it right, too early, too late, one misstep could
ruin the syncopated sound of double dutch lines

DARK, AND LOVELY, AND LIMITLESS

For Alice Walker

her story does not begin or end in february,
it cannot be celebrated, appreciated, and narrated
in twenty-eight short days for her beauty
is dark, and lovely, and limitless

she hails from purple mountains majesty
east african fields, her mother's land
draped in amethyst petals, leaves jaded
in velvet, crowns rooted in smoky quartz

she thrives despite being dormant,
buried underneath tiny granules,
surviving in sediment, parched soil
miseries from centuries of neglect

she paints to remain visible in low light,
splattered hues ranging from ink to iris,
her blackest moments canvassed in iron
and indigo, a portrait of her life in bloom

her story does not begin or end in february,
it cannot be celebrated, appreciated, and narrated
in twenty-eight short days for her name
is *saintpaulia ionantha*, an african violet

whose beauty is dark, and lovely, and limitless.

NO. 8

give me a pen, and i will write this pain away
you
resurfaced
inked
memories
you
carry
unhealed
wounds
you
and i will write this pain away, give me a pen

2023

AFRICAN AMERICAN READ-IN

SPECIAL GUEST

TARA CAMPBELL

THE DAILY MAD LIB

For Tara Campbell

good ███████ and thank you   [time of day]
for coming to this joint press conference.
my name is ████████ ███████.   [first name] [last name]
i am the ██████ of ████████ police   [law enforcement title] [town]
for ██████████ county,   [county]
here in the state of ██████.   [state]
on behalf of the officials standing
behind me representing local, state,
and federal law enforcement agencies,
we are saddened by the ████ events   [horrible synonym]
that occurred here today and offer our prayers
and deepest sympathies to the victims, their families,
and the entire █████████ community.   [repeat town]

here's what we know: at approximately ██:██ ██   [clock time] [am/pm]
our 911 emergency system received a call reporting ██   [number]
gunshots fired at a ██████████ in the ██████ district.   [public place] [district]
an officer nearby on an unrelated call responded
and was first to arrive at the scene of this ███████ tragedy.   [senseless synonym]
the assailant, a male approximately ██–██ years old,   [between 18 & 25] [50–65]
standing approximately ██' ██", weighing roughly   [5 or 6] [between 1&10]
██████ pounds, last seen wearing ██ clothing,   [150–200] [dark color]
a baseball cap, and tactical gear, carrying a █████,   [type of gun]
fled the scene in a ██████ ████████   [color] [type of car]
heading █████ on ████████████.   [direction] [name] [type of road]
it is with a heavy heart that i must report
██ gunshot victims died at the scene.   [<30]
details regarding the deceased will not be released
until next of kin have been properly notified.
██ were transported by ambulance to ██ area hospitals   [even # <20] [2–4]
in ███ and █████. ██ are in critical condition   [city] [town] [odd #]
and are being prepped for surgery. ██ are in stable   [even # <8]
condition and are expected to live. ██ sustained   [odd # <7]
non-life-threatening injuries and have been released.

71

a tip line has been set up for anyone with information
leading to the capture and arrest of the suspect.
if you see someone matching the shooter's description,
do not engage, he should be considered armed and
dangerous. call 1 (800) ██-██ immediately.   [seven digit #]

today's violence marks the country's ██st/nd/th mass killing   [# <25]
in 20█, according to an online database maintained by   [between 1 & 23]
several agencies. know we will not rest until this coward
is behind bars and justice is served so we in the great state
of ███████ and our ███████ nation can begin   [repeat state] [positive adj.]
to heal and recover. because this investigation
is ongoing, we are unable to answer any questions,
disclose any other information, or fill in any more blanks.

973.0496

you asterisked my voice, buried it in parchment, tomes too heavy to **lift**. **may** the black boxes, redacted gifts from ancestors, always be accessible to **me**.

write, they say, what upsets you, threatens you, paper moon scribbles, raising **up me** and others like me with bowed heads, clasped hands resisting earth's choke **hold**.

down bad beasts cataloguing and circulating a litany of isms and phobias onto **me in** hate so my eyes remain censored, plagued for centuries by maladies binding me **down**.

history, still rooted and written in hypocrisies, veiled in plain sight tragedies, to **keep with** tradition, rule of thumb trigger warnings where you ban, block, and burn **me**.

your voice weeding my colorful chapters from carrels and bookshelves, truths too **close**, **bitter** reminders to read what defines me, enshrines me, until my contents are **safe**.

twisted tales no longer archived, earmarked pages, cracked spines replacing hard truths **and lies**, yet still i rise, with pen in hand, ready to restore our libraries with a liberating **sound**.

NO. 9

pour my outrage onto the page before it corrodes me
reacting
judgmental
environmental
isms
reacting
deprecating
humiliating
phobias
reacting
to me on the page before my rage outpour corrodes it

2024

AFRICAN AMERICAN READ-IN

SPECIAL GUEST

E. ETHELBERT MILLER

THREE TERCETS TO REMEMBER

For E. Ethelbert Miller

before rosa there was claudette, young, gifted, and black
refusing to move from the front of the bus to the back
not even sojourner and harriet could prevent her attack.

before jackie there was satchel aka leroy robert paige
birmingham's black baron blurring color lines, at age
59 still throwing strikes from the major's center stage.

before nikki there was phillis, named after the slave ship
that carried her to a nation where she escaped the whip
lashings written across backs because she learned to script.

RUN THE "GAMBIT"

dear america-

the time is 6:43 am or seventeen minutes before the top
of the hour. that's not a fire truck alarm blaring in the
background. it's not a police siren flashing blue then red.
it's not even the incessant chirping from your combo
smoke detector carbon monoxide monitor ringing in
your ears. it's actually your body's internal clock. telling
you to wake up. reminding you to wake up. begging and
pleading with you to wake up, like dap aka laurence
fishburne running across the campus yard in spike lee's
1988 movie *school daze*.

wake up because your eyes need to be open.
wake up because the enemy king is winning right now.
wake up because you miss a lot when you hit the snooze button.
wake up because everything isn't black or white.
wake up because bad things happen
          when you ignore right from wrong.
wake up because only a fool's mate wastes precious seconds.
wake up because enough is enough.
wake up because a draw won't do this time.
wake up because you will have plenty of time
          to sleep when you're dead.
wake up because there are no lucky colors.
wake up because you are sleeping through
          this game called life.
wake up because your pawns are being knocked
          on their sides and pushed to the edge.
wake up because time is not the gift that keeps on ticking.
wake up because your queens are being sacrificed.
wake up because you need to rub the isms
          from the corners of your eyes.

wake up because everything can't be identified
	by checking or moving one square.
wake up because the last amber waves of grain
	are falling through the hourglass.
wake up america before the face across from you says checkmate!

sincerely,
a chorus of your woke citizens

NO. 10

there is no difference between a poem and a prayer
when
life
throws
curves
when
relief
saves
you
when
there is no difference between a prayer and a poem

2025

AFRICAN AMERICAN READ-IN

SPECIAL GUEST

TERI ELLEN CROSS DAVIS

FSBO: 5416 SECOND STREET, NORTHWEST

For Teri Ellen Cross Davis

this 1,332-square-foot 1935 brick row house, centrally
located in the sought-after petworth neighborhood
of our nation's capital, could be yours, this one-of-a-kind gem
dripping in historic charm, just a stone's throw from jefferson
street, once belonged to elizabeth, my grandmother, my mother's
mother, the second residence she purchased, the first,
as a widower in the 1950s, caring for a family of six,
three boys & three girls, on a domestic's hourly wage
of one dollar & eighty-six cents.

the spacious upper level boasts three bedrooms
& two full bathrooms, ideal for her young family
then & perfect for yours now—decorated in nostalgia,
the solid oak wood floors & architectural molding framing
the parlor & dining room on the main level created
a warm inviting space for entertaining uncles, aunties,
cousins, family friends & church people. a finely
carved duncan phyfe & vintage dumbwaiter felt right
at home in this space adjacent to the rear galley kitchen,
walled in mustard yellow vintage appliances, formica
& natural light. the residence's lower level, expertly crafted
during the generation of children should be seen not heard,
features plenty of space to play ping-pong, dominos
& cards indoors (but never on sundays) & direct access
to the outdoors, the concrete backyard playground,
to shoot marbles, jump rope, hopscotch & dodge balls.

nestled in the heart of a vibrant pedestrian friendly
district, homeowners are steps away from public
transportation with easy access to an array of local
amenities throughout chocolate city, like peoples
drugstore, jackie lee's, hot shoppes & miles'-long
take along sandwich shops, the original doordash
uber eats from back in the day. nearby schools
include rudolph elementary (now barnard),
mcfarland junior high, roosevelt senior high
& howard university, the real hu where blackbyrds sing.

this motivated seller is looking for a buyer who values
community over new construction, not some investor
who wants to magically erase charm, replace not restore
surfaces, whitewash brown paneled walls in benjamin
moore's chantilly lace. this move-in ready home does not
need to be meticulously reimagined with renovated, sleek
modern surfaces, open-concept layouts, chef's kitchen
conveniences & sophisticated technology. what it needs
is a buyer committed to honoring & preserving the culture
of the district of columbia, someone who will care
for this home & her community, the way elizabeth,
my grandmother, my mother's mother, did for fifty years.

IN MEMORIAM

and despite it all
they still live on
hidden and buried
under a canopy
of white elms,
hundred-year-old
shadows of black roots
once known for guarding
one acre not forty,
a postage size parcel
of terra earth,
now prime real estate
for suburban strip malls
and sprouting parking lots
—and spacious new homes
for toyotas and teslas

and despite it all
they still live on
submerged and buried
in watery graves,
sunken ghost towns,
where log cabins
once stood proudly
now razed and replaced
with subsidized pine boxes
anchoring white sediment
and black grief,
haunting luxury lake
front communities
and their resident cruisers
and catamarans
who now trespass
dirt roads no longer walked

and despite it all
they still live on
veiled and buried
in the north hollow,
a mob of swirling winds
once carrying a thin red
line of flames to slash
and burn, and set ablaze
rosewoods and greenwoods,
and neighborhoods
of blackened streets,
ashes to ashes,
and dust to dust,
a nutrient-rich layer of land
newly cleared now ready
to fertilize and traffic
blue chips and stock bonds
for the wealthy transplants

and despite it all
this commonwealth
of indelible towns
population of the unknown,
tombs marked with numbers,
unfamiliar symbols,
birth and death bookends,
letters spelling recycled epithets
borrowed from family bibles
and masters still live on

as long as there is someone
to say their names

austin grove and bluemont
bowmantown and bull run valley
gainsboro and gleedsville
langston and lower sycolin
macsville and midway
oscarville and rock hill
saint louis and settlement
throughfare and upperville
vinegar hill and willard

they
still
live
on.

NO. 11

traveling down the road i was born to know
took
decades
navigating
detours
took
roundabouts
bypassing
dreams
took
down the road i was born to know traveling

POSTLUDE

ACKNOWLEDGMENTS

Many of the poems within *februaries* pay homage to writers from the Washington, D.C., metropolitan area who were special guests at the annual African American Read-In at Broad Run High School from 2015–2025.

2015
"to rewrite this world again" is an eintou that was inspired by language from "we be gods," "african whitney," and "so down to earth when she should be flying" from Tinesha Davis' *All Black Girls Ain't Got No Rhythm and other urban hymns* (Magic People Press, 2006). The eintou is an African American form consisting of seven lines.

"no. 1" is a skinny poem that incorporates a variation of a personal message inscribed inside a signed copy of Tinesha Davis' 2006 poetry collection. The skinny, created by Truth Thomas in 2005 at Howard University in a Tony Medina Poetry Workshop, is an eleven-line poem with a fixed form. Each skinny poem in *februaries* borrows a line or phrase from a tribute poet. They form the first and last lines of the skinny poems and while not always a direct quote, they are italicized to make them distinct and are recognized here.

2016
"at midnight, apartment 1 sits by the window, still waits for her ghost to come home" uses language from Le Hinton's poem "47th & Baltimore" from *The Language of Moisture and Light* (Iris G Press, 2014).

"swan song" incorporates phrases from James Weldon Johnson's 1900 poem "Lift Every Voice and Sing" and Samuel Francis Smith's 1831 poem "America," also known as "My Country, 'Tis of Thee."

"no. 2" borrows a line from Le Hinton's poem "Cards Flash Back" from his 2014 collection.

2017

"haiku blues" takes inspiration from "Blues Haiku For Big Maybelle" from Venus Thrash's *The Fateful Apple* (Hawkins Publishing Group, 2014). It also incorporates the titles from the following songs performed by Billie Holiday: "When You're Smiling," written by Larry Shay, Mark Fisher, and Joe Goodwin in 1928, "Them There Eyes," written by Maceo Pinkard, Doris Tauber, and William Tracey in 1930, "Pennies from Heaven," written by Johnny Burke in 1936, and "You Go to My Head," written by Haven Gillespie in 1938.

"iconic" uses the phrase "weary blues," which is from the title of the 1925 Langston Hughes poem "The Weary Blues."

"no. 3" borrows a line from Thrash's poem "A Different Key" from her 2014 collection.

2018

"an american girl" includes the Latin phrase "partus sequitur ventrem," which, when loosely translated, means "that which is born follows the womb," a 1662 Virginia law. It stated that a child's status was determined by their mother's status, not their father's, legally binding children to the enslaved status of their mother.

"no. 4" incorporates language from Brooke C. Obie's novel *Book of Addis: Cradled Embers* (For the People Press, 2016).

2019

"can i buy a vowel?" uses a line from Camisha Jones' poem "The Sound Barrier" from *Flare* (Finishing Line Press, 2017) as its epigraph, with permission from the author. Lines in the poem were also inspired by phrases from Jones' poems "Fibromyalgia: A Haiku," "Intercession," "Ode to My Hearing Aids," and "Tinnitus," all from *Flare*.

"no. 5" borrows a line from Jones' poem "My Anxieties Learn to Pray," also from *Flare*.

2020
"sugar plum" was inspired by the children's book *I Bet She Called Me Sugar Plum* (Franklin Street Gallery Productions, 2004) by Dr. Joanne V. Gabbin.

"no. 6" uses a line from the 2022 *Morgan Magazine* interview with Dr. Gabbin, "An Eponymous Honor" (magazine.morgan.edu/an-eponymous-honor).

2021
"enjambment" incorporates a phrase from "For Frank Sinatra" and "Thirteen Ways of Looking at a Pit Bull" by Reuben Jackson from *Scattered Clouds: New & Selected Poems* (Alan Squire Publishing, 2019).

"still" references musical artists Thelonious Monk, Edward Kennedy "Duke" Ellington, and Prince Nelson.

"no. 7" borrows a line from Jackson's poem "Elegy" from *My Specific Awe and Wonder* (Rootstock Publishing, 2024), published posthumously, and plays on the titles of Prince's songs "When Doves Cry" and "Purple Rain," both written by Prince and released in 1984.

2022
"no. 8" incorporates a quote from a 2022 Danny Queen interview with Dinahsta Thomas for Queen's Color Me Poetry YouTube channel (youtube.com/watch?v=-tcSAKdsXZA).

2023
"973.0496" is a double golden shovel using the title and language (bolded) of Maya Angelou's poem "Still I Rise" from *And Still I Rise* (Random House, 1978) and Rihanna's lyrics (bolded) from

"Lift Me Up" (written by Rihanna, Tems, and Ryan Coogler, released in 2022). The title "973.0496" references the call number used to catalogue books about African American history and culture. The golden shovel form was created by Terrance Hayes in his poem "The Golden Shovel" from *Lighthead* (National Geographic Books, 2010).

"no. 9" borrows a quote from the 2020 interview "Hybrid by Nature: A Conversation with Tara Campbell" on The Rumpus (therumpus.net/2020/07/29/the-rumpus-interview-with-tara-campbell).

2024
"three tercets to remember" takes inspiration from the title of E. Ethelbert Miller's poem "Two Tercets to Remember" (2014), which can be found online at poemhunter.com/poem/two-tercets-to-remember.

"run the 'gambit'" is an epistolary poem that references a scene from Spike Lee's 1988 movie *School Daze*.

"no. 10" uses language from Miller's poem "Salat" from *Whispers, Secrets & Promises* (Black Classic Press, 1998).

2025
"in memoriam" lists the names of historically black towns in Virginia.

"fsbo: 5416 second street, northwest" was inspired by Teri Ellen Cross Davis' poem "3939 Strandhill Road, Cleveland, Ohio" from *a more perfect Union* (Mad Creek Books, 2021). The Blackbyrds, mentioned in the poem, is a musical group formed by trumpeter Donald Byrd in 1973.

"no. 11" borrows a line from Teri Ellen Cross Davis' "Fade to Black" from *Haint* (Gival Press, 2016).

****

februaries was a 2024 semifinalist for the Marginalia Prize by Small Harbor Publishing. Thank you to the following journals and magazines for publishing earlier versions of some of the poems.

Spoken Black Girl Magazine, Issue 5: Motherhood, Spring 2024
"swan song"

Mid-Atlantic Review, May 2024
"dark, lovely, and limitless"

Porcupine Literary, August 2024
"973.0496"

The Fire Inside: Collected Stories & Poems from Zora's Den 3,
September 2024
"muse"

Gargoyle Magazine, March 2025
"an american girl, an abecedarian," "spiraling,"
"sugar plum," and "three tercets to remember"

IN GRATITUDE

February is my favorite month of the year for so many reasons. I was born in February. My husband and my two sons were also born in February. My daughter is the only one in the family not born in February. Four of my closest girlfriends were born in the second and shortest month of the year. Some of my favorite black writers, Langston Hughes, Toni Morrison, Audre Lorde, and Alice Walker, have February birthdays. And my debut poetry collection, *purl*, from Finishing Line Press, was published on February 14, 2025. For as long as I can remember, February has always been a month full of celebrations.

✳✳✳✳

Thank you to those visiting writers from Washington, D.C., Maryland, and Virginia (the DMV), who came to Broad Run High School and shared priceless anecdotes and advice to audiences of young readers and writers: Tinesha Davis, Venus Thrash, Le Hinton, Brooke C. Obie, Camisha L. Jones, Dr. Joanne V. Gabbin, Reuben Jackson, Dinahsta Thomas, Tara Campbell, E. Ethelbert Miller, and Teri Ellen Cross Davis. Thank you to the administration, staff, and student body of Broad Run; *februaries* would not exist without you. I have been so fortunate to work with so many wonderful educators throughout my teaching career. Special thanks to Amy Buckley, who was responsible for hosting the first read-in at Broad Run in 2015, and Bria Coleman, Sarah Dyer, Beth Konkoski, Barbara Musselman, Lauren Sacco, Sally Toner, and the English Department for helping to keep the tradition going for over a decade.

Thank you to Rowana Abbensetts-Dobson of *Spoken Black Girl Magazine*, Victoria Kennedy Adams of Zora's Den, Greg Luce of *Day Eight* and *Mid-Atlantic Review*, Richard Peabody of *Gargoyle Magazine*, and Hannah Grieco of *Porcupine Literary* for amplifying my voice and giving some of the poems in this chapbook their first homes.

Thank you to Rachel Coonce and Courtney Sexton of The Inner Loop and Casey Catherine Moore of Brookland's Busboys & Poets, for inviting me to read poems at literary events in the DMV.

Thank you to ARTWIFE, Books & Bounty, the Poetry Society of Virginia, Scribente Maternum, The Watering Hole, and The Writer's Center for supporting my writing journey through interviews, retreats, and workshops.

Thank you to Rowana Abbensetts-Dobson, Kenneth Carroll, Keith Gilyard, Hannah Grieco, Holly Karapetkova, and Monica Prince for spending time with *februaries* and writing generous blurbs.

Thank you to Annie Marhefka, Kapua Iao, Alexa Laharty, Ann Quinn, Melissa Nunez, Marylou Fusco, and the entire team at Yellow Arrow for publishing this chapbook and giving me another reason to love the month February.

Thank you to the Evans, Peterson, Matthews, Stancil, and Mosley families for your love and support. To my parents, Arthur and LaVarne, for being my first teachers. I am who I am because of you. To Shawn, Kennedy, Harrison, and Kendall for being my people. You are my everything. A special shout out to Harrison for (once again) creating art to grace the cover and a gallery of portraits to fill the interior pages.

Thank you to my extended family, friends, and fellow writers for championing me and this chapbook of poems.

Lastly, thank you to everyone who is committed to narrating, celebrating, and appreciating the life experiences and achievements of African Americans well beyond the twenty-eight days in February.

ABOUT THE ARTIST

Harrison Evans, a self-taught artist from Virginia, specializes in digital and body art. Working with a primarily monochromatic palette, he created the cover art for *purl* and *februaries*. Fueled by creativity and passion, this emerging illustrator aspires to use his art to enrich, educate, and empower those in his community and beyond.

ABOUT THE AUTHOR

Michele Evans is the author of the debut poetry collection *purl* (Finishing Line Press, 2025), which was nominated for the 2025 Maya Angelou Book Award. She is a fifth-generation Washingtonian (D.C.), writer, teacher, and adviser for *Unbound*, an award-winning Northern Virginia high school literary magazine. This Watering Hole Fellow and Teaching Consultant for the Northern Virginia Writing Project studied English at Smith College, King's College London, and the Graduate School at the University of Maryland. Her poems have appeared in *Artemis Journal, Bellevue Literary Review, Welter Magazine*, and elsewhere. She lives online at awordsmithie.com.

Thank you for supporting independent publishing.

Yellow Arrow Publishing is a nonprofit supporting writers and artists who identify as women. Visit YellowArrowPublishing.com for information on our publications, workshops, and writing opportunities.

www.ingramcontent.com/pod-product-compliance
Lightning Source LLC
Chambersburg PA
CBHW020418130626
46549CB00006B/2619